HOW TO SPEAK AND LISTEN EFFECTIVELY

The WorkSmart Series

The Basics of Business Writing
Commonsense Time Management
How to Speak and Listen Effectively
Successful Team Building

HOW TO SPEAK AND LISTEN EFFECTIVELY

HARVEY A. ROBBINS PH.D.

amacom

AMERICAN MANAGEMENT ASSOCIATION
THE WORKSMART SERIES

This book is available at a special
discount when ordered in bulk quantities.
For information, contact Special Sales Department,
AMACOM, a division of American Management Association,
135 West 50th Street, New York, NY 10020.

This publication is designed to provide accurate and authoritative
information in regard to the subject matter covered. It is sold with the
understanding that the publisher is not engaged in rendering legal,
accounting, or other professional service. If legal advice or other expert
assistance is required, the services of a competent professional person
should be sought.

Library of Congress Cataloging-in-Publication Data

Robbins, Harvey A.
    How to speak and listen effectively / Harvey A. Robbins.
       p.   cm.—(The WorkSmart series)
    ISBN 0-8144-7793-3
    1. Communication in management.   2. Communication in
organizations. I. Title. II. Series.
HD30.3.R6   1992
658.4'5—dc20   91-43327
                                                 CIP

Printing number

10 9 8 7

CONTENTS

PREFACE

Individual (and team) success in the work setting is greatly influenced by the quality of relationships that develop and the types of communication that take place. Effective communication exists when individuals work to communicate in ways that:

- Enhance trust and respect.
- Eliminate unintended roadblocks.

How to Speak and Listen Effectively is designed to offer you a practical approach to the communication process by increasing your awareness and understanding of what takes place in the process and by helping you develop and strengthen effective communication practices. The book is divided into four chapters:

- Chapter 1. Why Don't People Communicate Better? This chapter introduces what the communication gap is and explores why it occurs between people. The focus of this part is to help reduce the confusion that can develop between you and someone else, when you make assumptions about another person's intentions.

- Chapter 2. Eliminate the Negatives. This chapter helps you discover the major barriers that get in the way of effective communication: differences in people's perception of the world around them; and in the way they behave with one another. Just like the old song about "eliminating the negatives and accentuating the positives," this chapter and the next are designed to take a more in-depth look at building better communication techniques.

- Chapter 3. Accentuate the Positives. Like a ping-pong game, good communication bounces back and forth between people. You are both talking and listening at the same time. This chapter focuses on the techniques that will help you effectively send and receive clear messages. It will increase your awareness of the way you talk to others, help you become more intentional (direct) in your communications, and increase your ability to listen effectively to what others are trying to tell you.

• Chapter 4. Practice Makes Communicating Easier. The main focus of this chapter is to explore in detail the situations in which you will most likely use these communication skills. We will look specifically at communicating problems, criticism, positive reinforcement, and communicating upwards, downwards, and sideways. And we'll suggest that you take the self-evaluation after practicing your communication skills for three months.

CHAPTER 1

WHY DON'T PEOPLE COMMUNICATE BETTER?

What's important to us may not be what's important to someone else.

One of the first major steps to achieve more effective communication between people is to recognize and understand why misunderstandings occur in the first place and then learn how to minimize or avoid them. Understanding the "gap" that occurs during the communication process will help you reduce the confusion that can develop between you and someone else and clarify assumptions that you both have about each other's intentions.

Before discussing the interpersonal communication gap, let's start out with a brief communication self evaluation to see where your strengths and weaknesses are.

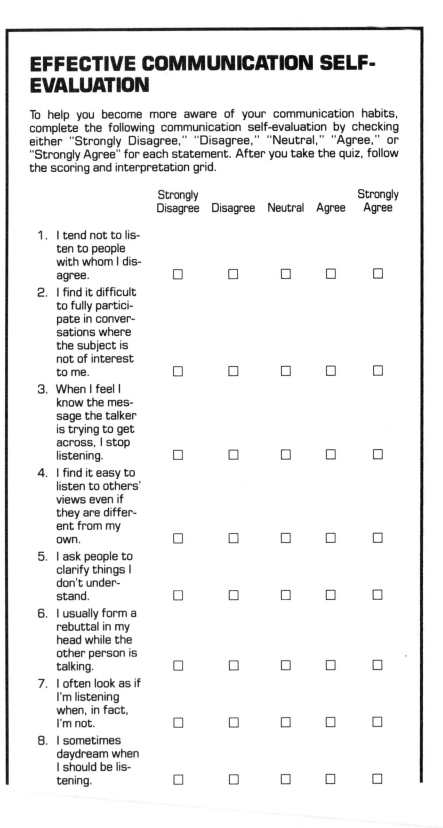

EFFECTIVE COMMUNICATION SELF-EVALUATION

To help you become more aware of your communication habits, complete the following communication self-evaluation by checking either "Strongly Disagree," "Disagree," "Neutral," "Agree," or "Strongly Agree" for each statement. After you take the quiz, follow the scoring and interpretation grid.

	Strongly Disagree	Disagree	Neutral	Agree	Strongly Agree
1. I tend not to listen to people with whom I disagree.	☐	☐	☐	☐	☐
2. I find it difficult to fully participate in conversations where the subject is not of interest to me.	☐	☐	☐	☐	☐
3. When I feel I know the message the talker is trying to get across, I stop listening.	☐	☐	☐	☐	☐
4. I find it easy to listen to others' views even if they are different from my own.	☐	☐	☐	☐	☐
5. I ask people to clarify things I don't understand.	☐	☐	☐	☐	☐
6. I usually form a rebuttal in my head while the other person is talking.	☐	☐	☐	☐	☐
7. I often look as if I'm listening when, in fact, I'm not.	☐	☐	☐	☐	☐
8. I sometimes daydream when I should be listening.	☐	☐	☐	☐	☐

	Strongly Disagree	Disagree	Neutral	Agree	Strongly Agree
9. If I'm not listening, I will tell the person.	☐	☐	☐	☐	☐
10. I listen for the main ideas, not the details.	☐	☐	☐	☐	☐
11. I recognize that words mean different things to different people.	☐	☐	☐	☐	☐
12. If I don't like or believe the other person, I block out what is being said.	☐	☐	☐	☐	☐
13. I look at the person who is talking.	☐	☐	☐	☐	☐
14. I concentrate on the other person's message rather than on physical appearance.	☐	☐	☐	☐	☐
15. I know which words and phrases cause me to react emotionally.	☐	☐	☐	☐	☐
16. I preplan my communications with others to accomplish my goals.	☐	☐	☐	☐	☐
17. I anticipate others' reactions to my communications.	☐	☐	☐	☐	☐
18. I take into consideration how others want to receive my information.	☐	☐	☐	☐	☐
19. I try to determine the mood of the other person (angry, frustrated, worried, etc.) when communicating with them.	☐	☐	☐	☐	☐

(continues)

	Strongly Disagree	Disagree	Neutral	Agree	Strongly Agree
20. I feel that I am able to communicate my ideas to others so that they understand my meaning.	☐	☐	☐	☐	☐
21. I often feel others should have known my meaning.	☐	☐	☐	☐	☐
22. I am able to receive negative feedback without getting defensive.	☐	☐	☐	☐	☐
23. I practice my listening skills on a regular basis.	☐	☐	☐	☐	☐
24. I find it hard to concentrate on what someone is saying when there are noise distractions.	☐	☐	☐	☐	☐
25. I often judge the content of others' messages when they're communicating with me.	☐	☐	☐	☐	☐
26. I restate information given to me to make sure that I understand it correctly.	☐	☐	☐	☐	☐
27. I let others know that I recognize the emotional level they are at when speaking to them.	☐	☐	☐	☐	☐

SCORING

Circle the number that corresponds to your checkmarks for each question. Then add up these numbers to reach a total score.

	Strongly Disagree	Disagree	Neutral	Agree	Strongly Agree
1.	5	4	3	2	1
2.	5	4	3	2	1
3.	5	4	3	2	1
4.	1	2	3	4	5
5.	1	2	3	4	5
6.	5	4	3	2	1
7.	5	4	3	2	1
8.	5	4	3	2	1
9.	1	2	3	4	5
10.	1	2	3	4	5
11.	1	2	3	4	5
12.	5	4	3	2	1
13.	1	2	3	4	5
14.	1	2	3	4	5
15.	1	2	3	4	5
16.	1	2	3	4	5
17.	1	2	3	4	5
18.	1	2	3	4	5
19.	1	2	3	4	5
20.	1	2	3	4	5
21.	5	4	3	2	1
22.	1	2	3	4	5
23.	1	2	3	4	5
24.	5	4	3	2	1
25.	5	4	3	2	1
26.	1	2	3	4	5
27.	1	2	3	4	5

Total = _____ _____ _____ _____ _____

Grand Total = ════════

ANALYSIS

Total Score

109–135   You have an excellent understanding of the communication process and use it effectively. Keep up the good work! A review of this book may be useful in helping you maintain your communication skills.

82–108   You have a strong understanding of the communication process and often use it effectively. You have a few areas that could use some work. Choose a particular communication weakness area and practice the skills outlined in the Communication Tool Box.

54–81   You have a general understanding of the communication process and may occasionally use it effectively. You frequently get into trouble when communicating with others and have a number of areas that could use some improvement.

27–53   You have many opportunities to improve your communication effectiveness. Your skills are not what they should be in order to consistently get your message across clearly to others. Others may frequently misunderstand your meaning.

FURTHER ANALYSIS

To further interpret the results of your communication self-evaluation and increase your awareness of your personal communication strengths and weaknesses, please answer the following questions:

1. On which questions did you score 1s? Scoring a 1 on any question indicates a specific communication weakness. There are recommendations in this book for overcoming each of your weaker areas.

   _____

   _____

   _____

2. On which questions did you score 5s? Scoring a 5 on any question indicates a specific communication strength. While it is important to improve upon your weaknesses, it is equally important to maintain your strengths. You will find recommendations in this book to help you keep up your communication strengths as well.

   _____

   _____

   _____

3. Based upon the information from the questions above, what are your communication strengths? What are the areas that you need to concentrate on to develop your communication skills? While you may have only circled a few 1s or 5s, any 2s and 4s you circled may also indicate a trend towards a particular communication strength or weakness.

   _____

   _____

   _____

4. What actions are you willing to take to reinforce your communication strengths and to improve in weaker areas? Start your plan of action with this question and add to it as you discover new strategies for becoming an effective communicator and as you read through this book.

_____

_____

_____

INTRODUCING THE INTERPERSONAL COMMUNICATION GAP

You don't always communicate what you intend to. Misunderstandings between people occur when the listener understands the message differently from the way the sender had intended it to come out. Just ask yourself two questions:

"I know you think you understand what you thought I said, but I'm not sure that what you heard is what I meant."

1. Have you felt offended by something someone either said or did to you over the last two weeks? Your answer is yes, isn't it?
2. Did you get up this morning, look bleary-eyed in the mirror and say to yourself, "I'm going to intentionally get someone angry today"? Your answer to this question is probably no, right?

So, why the difference? Well, chances are that the person who got you upset did not do it intentionally. You _assumed_ what his or her intentions were based on your negative reaction to his or her behavior.

(Text continues on page 12.)

Figure 1. Defining the interpersonal communication gap.

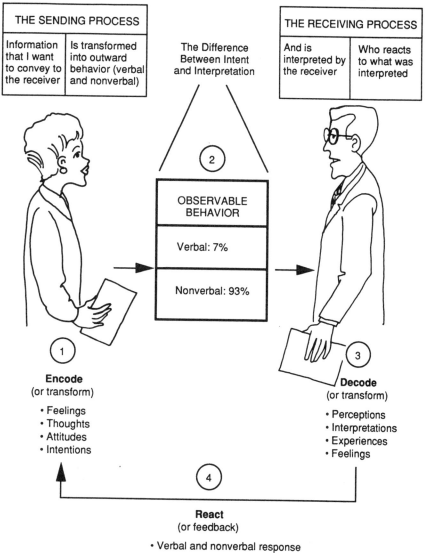

Figure 2.   Key points in the interpersonal communication gap.

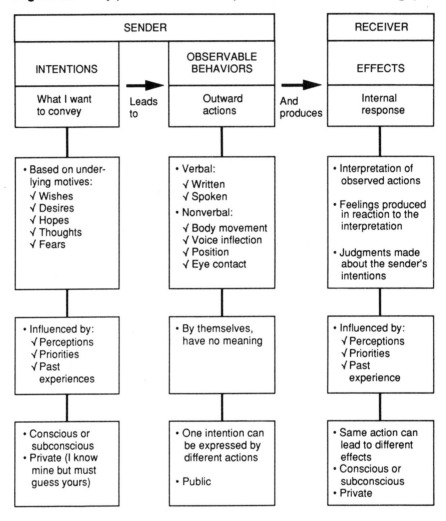

Figure 3. The gap in real-time examples.

SENDER		RECEIVER	
My Intention:	The Behavior I Show:	How I Interpret the Action:	My Internal Reaction:
• I want to show that I care about her.	• Pat her on the shoulder.	• She is patronizing me.	• I'm annoyed at you and feel "put down."
• I want him to recognize that I know a lot about this subject.	• Send him a 20-page document that I produced on the subject.	• He's too cautious and gets bogged down in details.	• I'm frustrated with his inability to "get to the point."
• I want her to tell me I'm doing a good job, but don't want to ask for the recognition.	• Talk with her about how much extra time I've been putting in on the projects.	• He's complaining about working too hard.	• I'm angry at him for not managing his time effectively.
• I want him to know how frustrated I feel when he makes decisions like that, but I don't want to jeopardize our relationship.	• Compliment the person on what a great job he does (and hope that it leads up to a discussion about his decision making).	• She really respects me for the type of work I do.	• I feel very positive about how well we work together.
• I wish he would tell me what to do.	• Ask him (daily): "Is there anything you'd like me to do?"	• He doesn't have enough work to keep himself busy.	• I'm frustrated with him because he doesn't show a lot of initiative.

DEFINING THE INTERPERSONAL COMMUNICATION GAP

Effective communi- cation exists between two people when the listener interprets the speaker's message the way the speaker intended.

Effective communication between two people exists when the receiver interprets the sender's message the way it was intended by the sender. An interpersonal communication gap occurs when the meaning of a message is interpreted and reacted to in a manner different from what was intended. You can see this illustrated in Figure 1, which shows how the sender encodes a message with observable behavior, which the receiver must decode. Since the majority of a message (93%) is comprised of nonverbal behavior—body position, tone of voice, and facial features—you can see how important it is to make sure that *how* you send a message is consistent with the message itself.

The meaning of a message (as conveyed by outward behavior) results from how the sender's intention is interpreted by the receiver as illustrated in Figure 2. For some real-time examples of how this gap works, consider the sender/receiver interpretations in Figure 3.

CHAPTER 2

ELIMINATE THE NEGATIVES

On a daily basis you probably encounter barriers when trying to communicate effectively with others. There are six common barriers along the road to communicating better. They distort the messages we hear and make it more difficult to communicate effectively with others.

1. *Hearing what you expect to hear.* How many of us have gone into meetings expecting to hear one thing and come out saying "See, I told you so," only to hear someone else interpret the same message totally differently. As human beings, we have this tendency to selectively listen for only those things that meet our expectations. We screen out everything else. This is why different people (with different expectations) hear different messages from the same speech. This is why politicians are intentionally vague . . . they can meet everyone's expectations!

2. *Evaluating the source.* Have you ever received one incorrect piece of information from someone and labeled your source "unreliable"? As a result, from that moment on, you evaluate any information coming from that person with a certain amount of doubt. On the other hand, when information comes from someone with an outstanding reputation, you often feel that the information cannot be questioned. In other words, you evaluate the source of the information to determine its value.

3. *Having different perceptions.* You've heard the story of the young boy who, after watching a baseball game, walked up to the three umpires and asked them how they call balls and strikes. The first umpire said, "Well, some's balls and some's strikes, and I calls 'em as I sees 'em." The second umpire said,

"Well, some's balls and some's strikes, and I calls 'em as they are." The third umpire said, "Well, some's balls and some's strikes, but they ain't nothin' till I calls 'em." The moral of the story? Not everyone is like you. If you assume that all people see the world as you do, then you're likely to be wrong about three-quarters of the time. We will look at the subject of perception in greater detail in the section on perceptual differences.

4. *Having different intentions.* When we see a person behaving or communicating in a certain way, we automatically read an intention in their actions. If, for example, you are upset with the way someone is communicating with you, you probably assume that the other party wanted to get you upset. Chances are, however, that this person wasn't even thinking of how you would react and was just communicating in a way that was comfortable to him or her.

5. *Ignoring nonverbal communications.* Be aware of the nonverbal signals people send when communicating, but also be aware that not all nonverbal signals are accurately interpreted. Take, for example, people who cross their arms and legs in order to concentrate better. Many books on nonverbal attitudes will tell you that this behavior means the listener is "tuning out." Baloney. One needs to be sensitive to both the verbal and nonverbal messages being sent and to their meaning. We will discuss this in more detail in Chapter 3.

6. *Being distracted by noise.* Do you concentrate and communicate effectively when there is a lot of noise around? It's doubtful. It is nearly impossible to tune out all the other conversations and associated noises that surround us daily. To be able to better send and receive messages from others, it's preferable to find a quiet place to conduct business. Some companies have installed noise barriers to enhance communication.

These barriers are the result of natural differences in the way people view the world and in the way they interact with one another. This chapter reviews the perceptual, behavioral, and verbal pattern differences that occur between individuals and provides some suggestions for overcoming them.

The most powerful word in the English language is _notice_. If you don't notice your environment, you can't interact effectively with it.

PERCEPTUAL DIFFERENCES

How we perceive our world can be viewed in three ways: how we select, organize, and interpret information (see Figure 4).

Information Is Selected

We are constantly surrounded and bombarded by activity. Lights, noise, talking, wind, and even our own thinking are sources of stimulation that we can perceive. To make sense out of things, we become selective in our perceptions. We block out the sound of buzzing lights, noisy conversations, or of a child asking for our help and concentrate on what we are reading. When the child finally does get our attention, we say, "Sorry, I didn't hear you."

We select the stimulation that we wish to perceive, based on our expectations, our needs, and our wants. For example:

- If our first impression of someone is negative, we tend to pick out those actions that support our first impression. We expect certain things to be true—and we find them.
- If we need more office space, we begin to notice all the wasted space in the building that we hadn't noticed before.
- If we want a new boat, all of a sudden we become aware of all the boats for sale along the road on our way home from work.

Information Is Organized

Once we have selected what we wish to perceive, we organize it. One way we organize is by "figure-ground" (see Figure 4). That is, one set of information becomes the "figure" we concentrate on and everything else becomes "background."

That's where a lot of misunderstandings start: two people having a conversation thinking they're talking about the same thing (the same figure) but, in reality, are talking about two different subjects (one about the figure, the other about the

Figure 4. Perceptions.

Perceptions are the result of the process of selecting, organizing, and interpreting observable behaviors. How we perceive things, or the effect that an action has on us, is private. Our perceptions are known only to ourselves until we communicate them to others. To communicate our perceptions, we must translate our intentions into actions and messages that others in their turn can observe and perceive. Our perceptions determine what our reality is. And unless we are aware of them, perceptions can become a major source of interpersonal gaps. The following summarizes key points about how individual perceptions are created.

PROCESS	HOW	WHY	EXAMPLE
① **SELECT STIMULI**	• Make choices on where to focus our attention. • Block out some stimuli.	• Influenced by: √ expectations √ needs √ wants	• I have to make a decision on whether or not to use a vendor by 5:00 P.M. In order to concentrate on analyzing the proposal, I block out the noise of the construction in the office next door, the voices of people talking in the hallway, and the secretary who is asking me a question. When the secretary finally gets my attention, I say, "Sorry, I didn't hear you."
② **ORGANIZE DATA**	• Use "figure-ground" organization: √ concentrate on one set of stimuli (i.e., "figure") √ place the rest into the background (i.e., "ground") • Use "closure" organization: √ see only a part of what's going on √ fill in what's missing (usually with negatives)	• Don't see what's in the background. • Can't see "figure" and "ground" at the same time. • Parts filled in are as real as what is actually observed.	• I need to talk with Joe this afternoon. As I walk down the hall, I see Joe walking with three other people. After the fact, I couldn't have told you who Joe was with in the hallway. • Someone overheard me talking about one of our vendor's plans to drop one of their product lines. By the end of the week, a rumor was running through my department that we were going to be dropping one of our products and laying people off. I have been trying to correct the rumor, but people are convinced that I'm not being "straight" with them.
③ **INTERPRET SITUATIONS**	• Make a value judgment about the situation.	• Influenced by: √ ambiguity of the situation √ attitude √ comfort zone (past experience, your personality) √ psychological context	• Bill is from the "Iron Range" (i.e., of all the available data I have on Bill, I have chosen to concentrate on where he is from). • "Rangers" are rowdy, drink, and aren't refined (i.e., I have chosen to think of a stereotype). • I don't want Bill on my team (i.e., I have made a judgment about Bill based on my perceptions).

People will sit up and take notice of you if you sit up and take notice of what makes them sit up and take notice.

background). This is sometimes known as a *dual monologue*. The speakers keep missing each other's points.

Has this situation ever happened to you? Describe the event here:

———————————————————————————

———————————————————————————

———————————————————————————

———————————————————————————

Having a dual monologue with someone is pretty frustrating, isn't it? To overcome this figure-ground issue, try to clarify with the other person up front the topic and desired outcome of your conversation.

A second way in which we organize information is through "closure" (see Figure 4). Closure is based on the principle that we, as human beings, tend to fill in missing pieces of information in our environments. This is not a new concept, but we have a natural tendency to fill in these blanks with *negative thoughts,* not positive ones. For example, if we are left out of a meeting or off a memo we feel we should have received, we feel that the sender intentionally tried to slight us. Sound familiar?

When was the last time you were left out of the information flow? How did you feel about the person who you think should have included you? What did you do? (Most likely, you got angry or got even in some way.)

———————————————————————————

———————————————————————————

———————————————————————————

———————————————————————————

When we assume negative intentions on another's part, we react by "getting even." This is called *inter-personal reciprocity.*

Many times we see only a part of what is going on but will organize it by filling in what is missing. The parts we fill in are as real to us as those which we have actually observed. This is why rumors are so easy to start, so powerful once they have started, and so hard to put an end to. The best way to overcome this tendency of filling in the blanks with negative assumptions is to check out the facts or ask for the other person's intentions the next time you start feeling upset about what someone is communicating to you.

Information Is Interpreted

Our interpretations of information are affected by the ambiguity of a situation, our attitudes, our comfort zone, and the psychological context of that particular situation (see Figure 4). Here are some examples:

Ambiguity

A man who is obviously in a hurry runs into an airport bar. He orders a drink, drinks it down, throws a $5 bill on the bar, and runs out. The bartender slowly walks up to the bar, picks up the money, turns to another patron and says, "Isn't that interesting? He was in such a hurry, he forgot to pay for his drink, but he left me a $5 tip." Ambiguity. The bartender interpreted the actions of the patron based on what was important to him or her. If you don't tell people how you want your information interpreted, he or she is free to interpret it based on whatever is important to them at the time.

Can you think of a time when you were in an ambiguous situation? What did you do? I'll bet you felt somewhat confused and needed to clarify what happened and sort out the details in order to feel that you had a handle on the situation.

_____

_____

_____

_____

How things look outside of us depends a lot on how things are inside of us.

Attitude

If you are like most people, your mood changes during the day based upon your interactions with other people or information. You may know what your attitude is at the time, but others do not. In order to enhance your communications with others, since they are interpreting your messages based upon both your verbal and nonverbal behaviors, you need to let them know what your attitude is at the time of your conversation. Some people play cartoonist on a 4- by 4-inch piece of cardboard, drawing a "Mister Happy" face on one side and a "Mister Yuk" face on the other, then hanging it outside their work space. As their mood changes during the day, they flip the card back and forth letting it act as a visual mood barometer to anyone coming in to talk.

Write down an example of when your attitude/mood shifted recently at work and how it affected your communications with others.

_____

_____

_____

_____

Sometimes when your mood shifts, others do not pick it up as quickly as you would like them to. Most likely, they will seem confused about how to interpret your message.

Comfort Zone

We all have our comfort zones. These usually are the result of where we grew up (northerners vs. southerners), our religious or philosophical background (Jewish, Catholic, Protestant, humanist, Moslem, atheist, etc.), our education and profession (MBAs, Ph.D.s, engineers, writers, salespeople, etc.), our cultural heritage (Italian American, African American, Latin American, Native American, etc.), sexual preferences (heterosexual, homosexual, both, neither, etc.). Your comfort zone is unique and makes you who you are. It also requires you to be sensitive to others' comfort zones if you want to communicate more effectively with them.

Pick an individual with whom you work. List as many comfort zones as you can think of for this person. Now, do the same for yourself.

_____	_____
_____	_____
_____	_____
_____	_____
_____	_____

Does this help you gain an understanding of where the other person is coming from?

Psychological Context

We all interpret information based upon the last piece of information we happened to be thinking about. For example, if a salesperson is thinking that she knows what a customer needs, she may write up the order this way, not the way the customer said he wanted it: She will have written the order based on her interpretation, not on reality. From time to time you get caught up in your own thoughts and don't pay attention to what another person is trying to tell you. It has been said that about 40 percent of the cost of redoing work is a result of mistakes made because of psychological context.

When was the last time you made a mistake because you wrote down what you were thinking, not what you heard? Give examples.

_____

_____

_____

_____

Misunder-standings between people often occur simply because two individuals are communi-cating on two different wavelengths. How you communi-cate with others—as both a sender and receiver of messages—will in large part be influenced by your own behavioral style.

How much sense does it make to pay attention to what others are saying as opposed to what you are thinking at the time? Checking out the accuracy of what you think you heard is most important in order to clear some of the barriers to more effective communication. Your increased sensitivity to perceptual differences will help you better understand and overcome behavioral and verbal differences.

BEHAVIORAL STYLE DIFFERENCES

What is important to you as an individual, in terms of the type of information you wish to send and are willing to hear, may not be as important to the person you are communicating with. He or she may have a different set of preferences in choosing how to receive information. It doesn't mean that either of you is necessarily wrong in defining what's "important," it simply means that there is a difference in your preferences in the way you send and receive information.

To be an effective communicator, you need to:

1. Understand your own style.
2. Diagnose the informational needs of others.
3. Communicate with others in a way that is sensitive to and aware of their informational needs.

The more information you have about how you communicate, as well as how others communicate, the easier it will be to "bridge the gap" that occurs as a result of differences in styles or informational preferences. (The material in this section is derived from the pioneering efforts in the field of interpersonal relationships and behavioral style of Dr. David Merril, Tracom, Denver.) To become more familiar with different behavioral styles, do the exercise that follows.

Behavioral Style Characteristics

Each different behavioral style exhibits different predominant characteristics. Figure 5 outlines the key values and comfort

(Text continues on page 24.)

Figure 5. Behavioral style model.

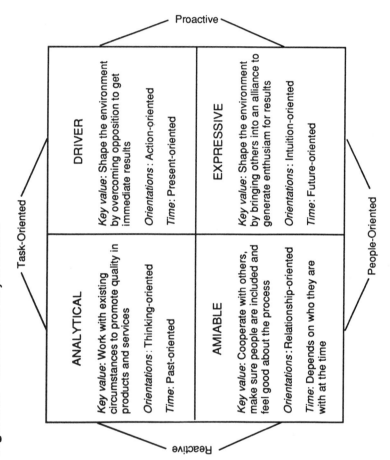

Proactive

Task-Oriented

People-Oriented

Reactive

DRIVER

Key value: Shape the environment by overcoming opposition to get immediate results

Orientations: Action-oriented

Time: Present-oriented

EXPRESSIVE

Key value: Shape the environment by bringing others into an alliance to generate enthusiam for results

Orientations: Intuition-oriented

Time: Future-oriented

ANALYTICAL

Key value: Work with existing circumstances to promote quality in products and services

Orientations: Thinking-oriented

Time: Past-oriented

AMIABLE

Key value: Cooperate with others, make sure people are included and feel good about the process

Orientations: Relationship-oriented

Time: Depends on who they are with at the time

EXERCISE: BEHAVIORAL STYLE WORDLIST

This exercise is designed to help you determine what your behavioral style is. Circle all the words below that you feel describe your behavior when you are *at work*.

Critical	Industrious	Pushy	Strong-Willed
Indecisive	Persistent	Severe	Independent
Stuffy	Serious	Tough	Practical
Picky	Expecting	Dominating	Decisive
Moralistic	Orderly	Harsh	Efficient
Aloof	Thoughtful	Cold	Goal-Oriented
Conforming	Supportive	Manipulating	Ambitious
Unsure	Respectful	Excitable	Stimulating
Ingratiating	Willing	Undisciplined	Enthusiastic
Dependent	Dependable	Reacting	Dramatic
Awkward	Agreeable	Egotistical	Friendly
Wishy-washy	Approachable	Flaky	Creative

After you have finished, draw a line down the middle and one side to side (dividing the wordlist into four equal rectangles). In which of the four corners are the most words circled? By comparing your quartile with the graph on page 16, you will be able to determine what your primary and secondary styles are.

zones of four styles of interpersonal behavior. Each style provides a unique view of one's environment. The styles are not good or bad—they are just different.

Learning the characteristics of each style will help you communicate effectively with people, enabling you to determine who fits what style category.

Analyticals. Analytical people have a tendency towards perfectionism. They deal with facts, data, logic, details. They are sometimes slow to make decisions because they want to be sure they know what they want before taking action. As a result, they may appear overly cautious and not good risk-takers. On the other hand, the decisions and information they provide is usually accurate and thoughtful. Feelings and emotions are kept inside and not revealed to others.

List those people you know who you feel fall into this category or show these characteristics and then describe their behavior.

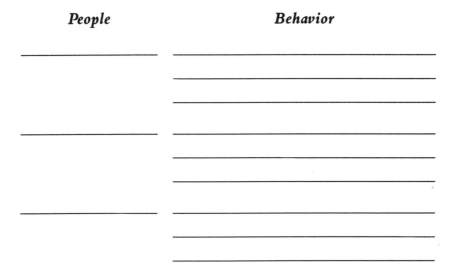

People	*Behavior*
_____	_____
	_____
	_____
_____	_____
	_____
	_____
_____	_____
	_____
	_____

Amiables. Amiables are the "warm fuzzies" of the world. People and friendships mean the most to them. They like to get people involved in any activities and are usually good at recruiting others as well as juggling multiple tasks. They are genuinely concerned with the feelings of others and go out of their way not to offend. They are just as opinionated as those on the right side of the model, but they are not as inclined to tell you what is on their mind. Amiables send out lots of cards for all occasions and are personally hurt or offended when others don't show similar consideration.

List those people you know who you feel fall into this category or show these characteristics and then describe their behavior.

People	*Behavior*
_____	_____
	_____
	_____
_____	_____
	_____
	_____
_____	_____
	_____
	_____

Drivers. Drivers are strong, decisive, results-oriented types. They provide strong guidance for those who need it (and, unfortunately, for those who do not). They can appear to be overly pushy at times, demanding of themselves and of others. Like the Analyticals, Drivers tend to keep their emotions to themselves, are highly self-critical, and resent those who waste their time with idle chit-chat and nonbusiness-oriented gossip.

List those people you know who you feel fall into this category or show these characteristics and then describe their behavior.

People	*Behavior*
_____	_____
	_____
	_____

People   **Behavior**

_____   _____

                             _____

                             _____

_____   _____

                             _____

                             _____

Expressives. Expressives are the party people. They love to have a good time, are highly enthusiastic and creative, and operate primarily by intuition. They have little tolerance for those who are not like themselves and find it a great sacrifice to have to put up with them. Because Expressives are easily bored and creative, keeping them on a task is a task in itself. They have a tendency to go off on tangents and, as a result, often seem somewhat "flaky."

List those people you know who you feel fall into this category or show these characteristics and then describe their behavior.

People   **Behavior**

_____   _____

                             _____

                             _____

_____   _____

                             _____

_____   _____

                             _____

                             _____

Now that you have completed this section, do the following exercise to determine what your preferred communication style is.

Toxic Relationships

There is a natural hostility that can build up between certain behavioral types that makes communication difficult at best. This natural tension occurs between individuals whose orientations are so dramatically different from one another that it often looks as if each is intentionally trying to get the other upset. For example, when an Analytical and an Expressive are trying to communicate, the Analytical will demand details that the Expressive is both unwilling and unable to provide (they just don't think in terms of details). Similarly, Expressives will want to talk about "the big picture" or some future considerations with a Driver whose only concern is for the work that has to get done today (read yesterday).

The typical toxic relationships are Analytical–Expressive, Driver–Amiable, and Driver–Expressive. (Conversely, the most compatible types are Driver–Analytical, Analytical–Amiable, and Amiable–Expressive.) To communicate effectively with different styles, it is important to understand their orientation, value it like your own, and learn some basic techniques to communicate within their comfort zone. The next section will help you achieve just this.

(Text continues on page 31.)

EXERCISE: IDENTIFY YOUR PREFERRED COMMUNICATION STYLE

Earlier in this chapter, you circled several words that describe how you see yourself. These words, along with the style descriptions, are clues for identifying your preferred behavioral/communication style *in the work setting*.

Based on this information, what is your preferred behavioral style(s) and what behavior do you exhibit that justifies your choice?

Your Behavioral   *Behavior*
Style

_____   _____

                    _____

                    _____

                    _____

To better understand your style preference, please respond to the following questions:

1. What significant events in your life may have helped create your preference for this style? Think of situations when your behavior really reflected the style.

   _____

   _____

   _____

   _____

   _____

2. What aspects of your preferred style cause you to feel good about yourself? Why?

_____

_____

_____

_____

_____

3. What aspects of your preferred style would you like to change? Why?

_____

_____

_____

_____

_____

4. What things about your preferred style do you dislike but are willing to accept? Why?

_____

_____

_____

_____

_____

5. Review again the words from the wordlist that you circled and the quadrant they represent. Which of the words reflect your behavior during times when you have been successful. Which reflect your behavior during times when you have been unsuccessful? Identify the words you selected and briefly describe what happened.

Words: _____

_____

(continues)

Successful: _____

_____

Words: _____

_____

Unsuccessful: _____

_____

6. In order to have stronger working relationships with others, what do people need to learn about you? How will you communicate this information?

_____

_____

_____

_____

_____

7. Review the behavioral styles that are *not* your preferred style. Which of the characteristics (for each of those styles) do you find difficult to accept in others? Why?

_____

_____

_____

_____

_____

8. Which of the characteristics (for each of the styles that are your nonpreferred styles) would help you be more successful than you are today? Why?

_____

_____

_____

_____

_____

Tips for Communicating Better With Different Styles

Review the list of tips in the checklist that follows and write down at least two that you can experiment with right away for each type.

With Drivers, try to:

- Be brief, specific, and to the point. Use time efficiently.
- Stick to business. Don't chit-chat.
- Come prepared with all necessary requirements, objectives, and support materials in a well-organized "package."
- Plan your presentation to present the facts cleanly and logically.
- Ask specific (preferably "what") questions.
- Provide alternative solutions and let them make the decision.
- If you disagree, take issue with the facts, not the person.
- If you agree, support the results, *and* the person.
- Persuade by referring to the objectives and results—the outcomes.
- After talking business, leave quickly—don't linger.

With Drivers, try not to:

- Ramble on or waste their time.
- Build up a personal relationship unless they initiate it.
- Be disorganized or messy.
- Leave loopholes or cloudy issues.
- Ask rhetorical or unanswerable questions.
- Come with predetermined decisions. Don't make decisions for them.
- Speculate wildly or offer unsubstantiated guarantees.
- Let your disagreement reflect on them personally.
- Reinforce your agreement with "I'm with you." They usually don't care.
- Direct them or order them around. They will rebel.

What two tips can you try out right away? How will you know whether or not you are successful?

_____

_____

_____

_____

With Expressives, try to:

- Plan the interaction to support their hopes, dreams, and intentions.
- Use the time to be entertaining, stimulating, fun, and fast moving.
- Leave time for socializing.
- Talk about their goals and what they find stimulating.
- Deal with the "big picture," not the petty details.
- Ask for their opinions and ideas.
- Provide ideas and concepts for implementing any necessary actions.
- Provide supporting examples from people they see as important.
- Offer special deals, extras, and incentives.

With Expressives, try not to:

- Legislate.
- Be cold, aloof, or tight-lipped.
- Drive on to the facts and press for solutions.
- Deal with details, or put them in writing, or pin them down to actions.
- Talk to them about generalities.
- Leave things hanging in the air—or they will be left there.
- Dream with them if time is of the essence—or else you will lose time.
- Talk down to them.
- Be dogmatic.

What two tips can you try out right away? How will you know whether or not you are successful?

_____

_____

_____

_____

With Amiables, try to:

- Start with some personal comment to break the ice.
- Show sincere interest in them as people, find areas of common involvement, be candid and open.
- Listen and be responsive.
- Be nonthreatening, casual, and informal.
- Ask "how" questions to draw out their opinions.
- Watch out for hurt feelings and personal reasons if you disagree.
- Define individual contributions.
- Provide assurances and guarantees that their decision will minimize risk and harm to others.
- Provide back-up support.

With Amiables, try not to:

- Rush headlong into business or the agenda.
- Stick to business constantly.
- Force them to respond quickly to your objectives.
- Be domineering, demanding, or manipulating. Don't threaten.
- Debate about facts and figures. Amiables have a tendency to get lost or stop talking.
- Be patronizing.
- Be abrupt and rapid.
- Offer options and probabilities. Don't be vague.
- Offer assurances you can't live up to.
- Decide for them or they will lose the initiative.

What two tips can you try out right away? How will you know whether or not you are successful?

_____

_____

_____ —

_____

With Analyticals, try to:

- Prepare your case in advance. Be as accurate as you can.
- Be direct, stick to business.
- Support their principles and thoughtful approach. List pros and cons to any suggestions you make.
- Present specifics and do what you say you can do.
- Take your time, but be persistent.
- Draw up a scheduled approach (with timetable) to any action steps.
- Follow through if you agree.
- Make an organized presentation of your position if you disagree.
- Be accurate, realistic. Give them time to verify that you are reliable.
- Provide tangible practical evidence.
- Provide guarantees over a long period of time, but give options.

With Analyticals, try not to:

- Be disorganized or messy.
- Be casual, informal, or loud.
- Rush the decision-making process.
- Fail to follow through.
- Waste time.
- Leave things to chance.
- Provide personal incentives.
- Threaten, cajole, wheedle, coax, or whine.
- Use testimonials from others or unreliable sources.
- Use someone's opinion as evidence.
- Be manipulative.

What two tips can you try out right away? How will you know whether or not you are successful?

_____

_____

_____

_____

Versatility is the ability to communicate with someone else based upon the other person's comfort zone, the way in which the other person wants to communicate. The next exercise is designed to help you develop an action plan to become more versatile in your communication with a specific person.

After completing these exercises you can see how communication is affected by people's different perceptions of the world, and by different behavioral styles in communicating. An additional area you now need to look at is the different verbal patterns people use.

VERBAL PATTERN DIFFERENCES

Verbal patterns are comprised of the specific words that you both use and tune to. Each of us has a dominant pattern. These patterns fall into three caterogies:

1. *Audio*— If you have an audio pattern, you tune to and retain only the information that you hear. Example: someone talking to you.
2. *Visual*— If you have a visual pattern, you pick up on information that you see and read. Example: memos or textbooks.
3. *Kinesthetic*— If you have a kinesthetic pattern, you learn best when given the opportunity to try things out. Example: learning by hands-on experience to run a piece of equipment.

Each pattern is often associated with predominant feelings and temperaments (see Figure 6). Communication between pat-

(Text continues on page 41.)

EXERCISE: VERSATILITY

Now that you have completed this section, do the following exercise. It is designed to help you practice communicating effectively with people who have different styles from yours, to become more versatile. In each of the following situations describe how you would open, conduct, and close the conversation with a person who is an Analytical, Driver, Amiable, or Expressive.

Situation #1

You are a design engineer who has been working in collaboration with Pat from manufacturing on a new product. In the middle of the night you wake up with a brilliant idea, a revolutionary design breakthrough that would make the product work more efficiently. But you are not sure of its manufacturing feasibility.

You have set up a meeting today with Pat to talk about the idea. In the past, Pat has been skeptical about your brainstorms. Knowing Pat's tendency, how can you be versatile in your discussion?

If Pat were an Analytical:

How would you open the conversation?

_____

_____

_____

Example: Open up the conversation with a description of how in the past your ideas may not have been completely thought through, but that you have thoroughly analyzed this one.

How would you conduct the conversation?

_____

_____

_____

Example: Give details of your idea providing comparisons with other similar ones that have worked well in the past. Talk slowly and unemotionally. Ask for additional thoughts from her.

How would you end the conversation?

_____

_____

_____

Example: Ask Pat for another meeting to further discuss your idea. Let her think over your conversation and generate additional thoughts before your next meeting. During the next meeting both of you can talk about the possibility of making a decision on your idea.

If Pat were a Driver:

How would you open the conversation?

_____

_____

_____

How would you conduct the conversation?

_____

_____

_____

How would you end the conversation?

_____

_____

_____

(continues)

If Pat were an Amiable:

How would you open the conversation?

_____

_____

_____

How would you conduct the conversation?

_____

_____

_____

How would you end the conversation?

_____

_____

_____

If Pat were an Expressive:

How would you open the conversation?

_____

_____

_____

How would you conduct the conversation?

_____

_____

_____

How would you end the conversation?

_____

_____

_____

EXERCISE: PLANNING YOUR COMMUNICATIONS

1. Choose an individual with whom you would like to either start a positive relationship or enhance your existing relationship.

2. List the behavior that this person exhibits most of the time when dealing with you or others. What and how does the person say things, how does he or she act?

_____

_____

_____

3. Based upon this behavior, what do you think this person's primary communication style is?

_____

_____

_____

4. Based on your analysis, what kind of things are you going to say and do to "bridge the gap" with this person over the next several encounters?

_____

_____

_____

5. How will you know whether or not you have been successful?

_____

_____

_____

Figure 6. Verbal pattern characteristics.

VERBAL PATTERN	ORIENTATION	VALUES	VERBAL CLUES	EXAMPLES
AUDIO (HEARING)	• Words	• Logic • Reason • Concepts • Logical strategies and solutions	• Think • Ideas • Concepts • Analyze • Hear • Sound	• This sounds good to me. • Let me think about it. • Let's hear the numbers. • How do you like the idea? • It seems a logical move. • Here are the facts.
VISUAL (SEEING)	• Pictures	• Images • Symbols • Holistic strategies and solutions	• See • Picture • Look • Vision • Seek • Symmetry	• Look at it this way. • See what I mean? • We need a balance. • Give me the big picture. • He can't see the forest for the trees.
KINESTHETIC (TOUCHING)	• Experience	• Intuition • Insight • Perception How people feel about a change or decision	• Feel • Touch • Sense • Perceive • Emotion • Share	• You know what I mean. • How do you feel about it? • Our people won't go for it. • Let's keep in touch. • Would you share? • I'm not comfortable with it.

terns may be easy or difficult, depending on how well the interacting patterns can tune in to one another's frame of reference. For example, the two patterns that present the least compatibility are Audio and Kinesthetic. People with an Audio orientation may have difficulty understanding why Kinesthetic people are so emotional; and Kinesthetic persons may perceive Audio types as being cold, unfeeling, or uncaring. Audio persons tend not to be feeling-oriented and may often have trouble describing feelings, in part because they do not primarily lead their lives with thoughts about feelings in mind.

How you interpret verbal patterns influences your ability to understand people. By identifying someone's dominant verbal pattern, you will be on your way to more effective communication. You will learn about how that person thinks, and so, have some clues on how to effectively share your ideas and suggestions with him or her. Cuing into the dominant pattern of a speaker can help you listen and respond—in the speaker's language.

The following exercise will give you the opportunity to diagnose the verbal pattern of people in your work environment.

EXERCISE: RECOGNIZING VERBAL PATTERNS

Identify the verbal patterns of your boss, a coworker, and a subordinate and justify your choice by describing the words that they use.

	Verbal Pattern	Words Used
Boss		
Coworker		
Subordinate		

CHAPTER 3

ACCENTUATE THE POSITIVES

You cannot control how effectively others listen. But you do have control over how effectively you send the message.

You have gained an understanding of why sensitivity to the way another person wants to receive information from you is important. Now you must learn how to effectively communicate your message so as to reduce the other person's defensiveness and increase his or her receptivity to you.

HOW TO SEND CLEAR MESSAGES TO OTHERS

How you communicate to others can be the source of mutual understanding and positive action—or a source of frustration and misunderstanding. The knowledge and skills you develop in sending clearer messages can help you become more aware and intentional in your communications with others.

In the model shown in Figure 7, you will notice that effective communication consists of both sending clear messages and giving feedback. This is what is known as mutuality: the shared responsibility you and the other person have for ensuring clear and effective two-way communication.

The filters shown on the model consist of the barriers and personal differences you have been reading about so far. These are the factors that can get in our way and must be overcome in order to send *and* receive clear messages.

Effective communication takes place when persons communicating send clear messages that are direct (don't beat around the bush), specific (provide enough details so the other person knows what you are talking about), and nonpunishing (avoid

(Text continues on page 44.)

Figure 7. A model for effective communication.

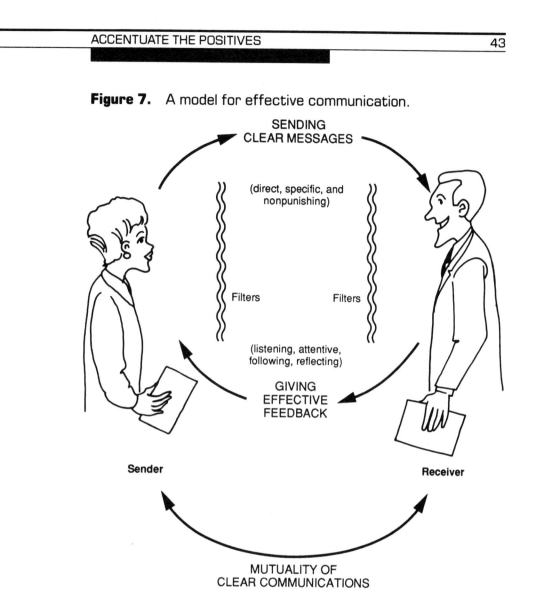

the use of anger or sarcasm when talking to someone else, otherwise he or she may stop listening). Each listens and gives feedback so the other person can be assured his or her message was received the way it was intended.

TECHNIQUES FOR EFFECTIVE COMMUNICATION

When you are trying to communicate clearly there are six techniques that can help you achieve success.

1. *Use feedback*. One way to make sure your message is getting through is to ask for feedback from the other person. In order to make sure your message got through the way you intended, ask:

> Did you understand the content and intention of what I just said?
> Do you agree with me?
> Do you want to add anything?

(How to give effective feedback is covered in more detail in this chapter under How to Become an Effective Listener.)

2. *Use multiple channels*. Use multiple simultaneous methods for getting your message across to another person, such as combining behavioral style and verbal pattern techniques. Since you may not be sure your message is being sent along a channel that is within the other person's comfort zone, you might want to send a message both verbally and in a follow-up memo, for example. Or you may want to provide a detailed history in the form of stories as background for decision making for a person who is an Analytical and a Visual. These are adequate comfort zones or pathways through which your message can be transmitted.

3. *Be sensitive to the receiver*. Try to pay attention to the receiver's behavior. Does the receiver make eye contact? Is there something different today in his or her communication pattern that was not evident yesterday?

Noticing people's communication patterns will help you determine whether they are receptive or not to your information and whether you need to approach them differently if they seem to have "tuned out."

When you do notice someone not listening to you, the best thing to do is gently acknowledge their inattention ("You seem to be preoccupied") and reschedule the conversation ("When would be a good time to come back?").

The last time you noticed someone obviously not paying attention to you when you were trying to communicate, what did you do to determine if the other person was receptive to you?

_____

_____

_____

_____

_____

4. *Be aware of symbolic meanings.* This is sometimes known as multicultural awareness. There are communication customs, which vary from one culture to another, that can lead to major misunderstandings. Symbolic meaning comes into play in our attitudes and in our choice of words. Since the English language often has multiple definitions for each word (sometimes as many as twenty-five different meanings), you may be sending messages using words with one meaning in mind (a slang definition for example) that are being received by someone else using a different meaning (a literal definition for example).

Have you ever run into a situation where cultural differences or different definitions for the same word created confusing communication? What happened? How were you able to finally clarify these differences? What would you do differently the next time this type of misunderstanding comes up?

_____

_____

_____

"But if he'd only listen, he'd know what I was trying to say!" "Sometimes I feel like she just doesn't hear me. Everything I say goes in one ear and out of the other!"

5. *Use simple language.* One of the biggest barriers to successful communication can be the use of jargon in our every-day conversations. We know how to use it, but few outside our specialty do. Since most people feel a bit embarrassed about asking for definitions, they feel left out. To overcome this tendency and open up communication, try to use basic common language that most people do understand. For example, instead of saying, "This individual displays a tendency towards a spectrum of deviate psychopathic anomalies," just say, "He's nuts!"

Give examples of recent situations where someone's use of their language was confusing to you. How did you attempt to clarify what they were saying?

_____

_____

_____

_____

_____

6. *Use repetition.* While repetitions can be annoying, by using them your message does have a better chance of getting through. Since we all tend to avoid acknowledging that we are not listening, it is best to repeat yourself until the other person acknowledges the message.

HOW TO BECOME AN EFFECTIVE LISTENER

How often are relationships in the work setting affected because people don't seem to really hear what others need to say? And how often are decisions made because of what people thought they heard versus what was really said?

Listening is perhaps the most challenging of the communication skills—and the most frequently ignored one. As a communicator, your effectiveness can be hampered or improved by how poorly or well you listen to others. Effective listening encourages clear and open communication between people. And through effective listening, you are able to more accurately understand and clarify others' intentions. Let's explore the listening process and review guidelines and techniques for enhancing listening effectiveness. Listening is one skill that, through practice, can be improved upon and strengthened. To begin, please take the time and complete the Listening Quiz.

Listening Efficiency

You may think you are able to listen efficiently to others. How much the average listener comprehends, however, may surprise you.

The consensus among researchers is that:

- Immediately following a speech, the average listener has comprehended approximately 50 percent of what he or she heard.
- Within 48 hours, the comprehension level has dropped to 25 percent or less.

Being able to listen efficiently and effectively is basic to your ability to communicate with others. While you are formally taught in school how to read, write, and speak, listening is a skill that you acquire informally. Look at Figure 8. It illustrates the percentage of time we spend in communication activities, as well as where we learned to write, read, speak, and listen. It is ironic that the areas in which we spend the most time and effort—listening and speaking—are the same areas in which we are least trained. Completing the next exercise will enable you to assess the negative impact poor listening can have.

(Text continues on page 49.)

LISTENING QUIZ

Mark each statement "True" or "False" based on your understanding of the listening process. Compare your answers with those at the end of the quiz.

1. People tend to expect or anticipate what they are familiar with. _____

2. Listening is an easy process. _____

3. Hearing and listening are the same thing. _____

4. For most people, it is easy to pay attention to a single topic for a long time. _____

5. The person talking has total responsibility for clearly getting his or her message across to others. _____

6. In the communication process, talking and listening are equally important. _____

7. It is easy to overcome distractions and listen effectively. _____

8. People usually pay attention to information that has personal meaning to them. _____

9. People usually hear what they expect to hear. _____

10. A person's background and experience determines to a large part what he or she hears. _____

11. Listening is a skill that can be learned.   _____

12. Listening is one of the easiest things to do.   _____

13. An effective listener pays atten-tion to both the verbal and non-verbal messages being sent.   _____

14. Listening shuts down when emo-tions run high.   _____

15. Being a good listener involves ar-guing the talker's points men-tally.   _____

Answers: 1. T; 2. F; 3. F; 4. F; 5. F; 6. T; 7. F; 8. T; 9. T; 10. T; 11. T; 12. F; 13. T; 14. T; 15. T

Don't worry about getting incorrect answers; effec-tive listening is not always as easy as it looks. Take a look at the answers that you got wrong and think about why the answers may be different from what you thought.

Guidelines for Listening Effectively

Effective listening is like a ping-pong match—you must have a good surface on which to play and learn to give and take easily. The physical setting creates this playing surface and either supports or detracts from the interaction that goes on between you and others. Creating an effective listening environment is critical if you want the other person to feel that his or her conversation with you is important. It involves setting the stage and becoming more receptive.

(*Text continues on page 51.*)

Figure 8. Our time investment in communicating.

COMMUNICATION				
Behavior				
	Writing	Reading	Speaking	Listening
	9%	16%	30%	45%
Training	K–12 grades and college	K–8 grades and special training	First three years of life and special training	?

Setting the Stage

1. *Minimize distractions.* It is difficult to turn off the sights and sounds of your environment. Depending on your interest level, you may become more or less distracted by the daily activity around you. This is natural but deadly to listening. If you cannot concentrate on what the other person is saying because you have too many other (more pressing) thoughts running through your mind, then stop the person from talking and reschedule the discussion. You can say something like, "I'm sorry, I'm preoccupied by other pressing matters. However, I'm interested in listening to you. Would it be O.K. if we rescheduled our discussion for, say, tomorrow morning?" If you are too distracted by external activities, conduct your discussion in a more isolated setting.

2. *Reduce any physical barriers.* Come out from behind your desk and sit next to the person you are talking to rather than using your desk as some sign of superiority.

3. *Avoid or limit interruptions.* Transfer your phone calls while you are having a conversation with somebody. Close the door to your office to restrict others from "popping in."

Becoming More Receptive

1. *Detect the central idea.* Sometimes it is difficult to determine what the other person is talking about. This is because people speak *while* they are thinking. They hope that you will be able to sort out the main message from the rest of their chaffe. In order not to lose interest in the speaker:

- Search for the central idea of his or her message.
- Evaluate all other information against this central idea.
- Pay attention only to the information relevant to the central idea, and forget about the rest. You may have to ask some probing questions in order to be sure you chose the correct central idea.

2. *Control your emotions.* As a human being, you are gifted with a wide and wonderful array of emotions (whether you

EXERCISE: THE COST OF POOR LISTENING

How can developing better listening skills be of any real value? The purpose of this exercise is to help you identify the impact, cost, and consequences of poor listening. Under each "cost" topic below, provide an example of the negative impact that poor listening can have.

Time: (Example: not listening to instructions causing you to redo something and losing time in the process)

_____

_____

_____

Money: (Example: not listening to financial advice)

_____

_____

_____

Relationships: (Example: breaking up with someone because he or she just "doesn't listen" to you)

_____

_____

_____

Productivity:

_____

_____

_____

Missed opportunities:

_____

_____

_____

Injury:

_____

_____

_____

Death:

_____

_____

_____

Lawsuits:

_____

_____

_____

Others:

_____

_____

_____

It is easy to see how important effective listening becomes when you think of the potential negative consequences of poor listening.

show them to others or not) that make life a bit more enjoyable. Unfortunately, these emotions sometimes act as barriers to listening effectively to others. The words you use or hear have a personal meaning to you. They stir up your emotions, sometimes positive ones, sometimes negative ones. In any case, you need to become more sensitive to the effects some words have upon your ability to listen. If you become emotional because someone uses a "red flag" word (one that stirs up negative feelings), you will probably tune them out, become defensive, and lose your ability to hear his or her message clearly. Complete the Red Flag Exercise to uncover your red-flag words.

EXERCISE: RED-FLAG WORDS

To determine what some of your emotionally charged words may be, look at the list of "red flag" words or phrases below. Check off all that stir up your emotions.

"You should/must . . ." ☐
Failure ☐
Feminist ☐
Chauvinist ☐
Sexist ☐
Arab ☐
Jew ☐
Moslem ☐
Atheist ☐
Catholic ☐
Protestant ☐
Loner ☐
Stupid ☐
"How many times have I told you . . ." ☐
Macho ☐
Homosexual ☐
Israel ☐
South Africa ☐
Sadam Hussein ☐
Communist ☐
Boris Yeltsin ☐
"You'll never . . ." ☐
"Why don't you . . ." ☐
"You never/always . . ." ☐
"You're wrong." ☐
Bad ☐

What other words would you add that stir up your emotions and interfere with your ability to listen to others? How do you overcome the emotions created by the use of these words?

_____

_____

_____

3. *Evaluate the message.* Since most people speak much slower than you are capable of listening to them, you have a tendency from time to time to let your mind wander. This leads to countless misunderstandings. In order to overcome this tendency and listen more effectively, spend the extra mental time evaluating what you are hearing. Argue the speaker's points mentally, taking into consideration the new information he or she is giving you.

Techniques for Active Listening

With a smooth environment in which to listen, the active process of give and take can begin. This active listening process can be broken down into two categories: nonverbal behavior and verbal behavior.

Nonverbal Behavior

Your physical position during communications tells the other person just how involved and interested you really are. In addition, your movement during the conversation shows interest or disinterest in what the person has to say. To improve nonverbal behavior,

- Maintain a relaxed yet alert posture.
- Be actively involved in the conversation.
- Minimize distracting gestures.
- Maintain effective eye contact (not staring, not looking away constantly).
- Acknowledge the other person nonverbally (head nods, smiles, etc.).
- Face the other person squarely instead of turning your head to the side to look at him or her.
- Maintain an open position (relaxed versus rigid placement of arms, hands, and head).
- Lean slightly towards the person instead of sitting stiffly upright or slouching back in your chair.
- Use gestures (especially when responding) but avoid dramatic hand waving, playing with pencils, or jabbing your finger at the person.
- Nod your head or smile.

AN EXTRA HINT ABOUT EYE CONTACT

While listening or talking to the other person, notice the size of the pupils of his or her eyes. Given even lighting, if he or she is attracted to you or your ideas, the pupils will get noticeably larger. If he or she is rejecting you or your ideas, they will get much smaller. If the pupils are dilated and fixed (also a symptom of death) and they are still breathing, then he or she is on a mental holiday. Their head may be bobbing up and down out of habit but they're not listening. You might as well stop talking and reschedule your conversation.

Can you think of others? Look at the Body Positioning Awareness Checklist after you write down a few:

_____

_____

_____

Silence allows you to organize your thoughts and encourages the other person to expand upon his or her ideas, reactions, or feelings. It also gives you time to think through what you have heard and how you may want to respond. Use silence after:

- Asking questions.
- Being asked a question.
- Important points have been made.
- Emotions are running high.
- You have received a large chunk of information at one time.

- Use eye contact to raise a question.
- Avoid the tendency to "jump in" before the other person has finished.
- Use nonverbal cues to prompt your interlocuter to provide more information.

Can you think of other occasions when using silence is advisable?

_____

_____

_____

Verbal Behavior

Verbal listening skills can be broken down into two kinds: probing/occasional questions and acknowledging/responding.

Probing and occasional questions can be used as door openers. Door openers are statements or questions that set the stage for

BODY POSITIONING AWARENESS CHECKLIST

To become more aware of the effects of your body positions on others, review the list below and place a checkmark next to those positions you feel create a positive reaction from others (he or she feels you are listening) when they are talking to you an *X* next to those you feel leave a negative impression, and an *N* next to those you feel are neutral.

_____ Smiling
_____ Sitting forward in your chair
_____ Frowning
_____ Rolling your eyes
_____ Withdrawing
_____ Not moving
_____ Hanging your head down or letting your head touch your shoulder
_____ Sighing
_____ Looking happy
_____ Scowling
_____ Shaking your head
_____ Folding your arms across your chest

_____ Narrowing your eyes
_____ Drumming your fingers
_____ Shrugging your shoulders
_____ Swishing your foot
_____ Bouncing your leg
_____ Puffing your cheeks
_____ Slumping in your chair
_____ Staring at the person
_____ Looking away constantly
_____ Playing with a pencil
_____ Nodding your head
_____ Looking critical
_____ Glancing at a clock

Can you think of other body movements that either enhance or restrict listening?

_____

_____

_____

the type of atmosphere that will exist during the discussion. They also encourage the other person to be more open and candid.

Occasional questions, asked during the conversation, tell the other person that you are interested in what he or she is saying. It allows the other person to give you more information and explain the situation in his or her own way.

To use probing and occasional questions effectively:

- Describe the other person's body language with statements such as "You look kind of excited about something" or "You seem frustrated."
- Offer a nonthreatening invitation to talk.
- Use brief encounters to initiate a conversation ("I've got some time around 2:30, would you like to talk about . . .").
- Ask one question at a time.
- Allow time for the person to answer fully.
- Ask open-ended questions (where a person must respond in longer sentences rather than just one word such as yes or no).
- Use verbal invitations such as "mm-hm." "Tell me more." "Oh?" "For instance?" "Then what happened?" "Really?" "And?"
- Avoid stringing questions together. Avoid playing "twenty questions" or sounding as if you're interrogating your interlocutor.
- Be sensitive to the other person's signs of defensiveness.

Acknowledging and responding fall into three categories: paraphrasing, perception checking, and summarizing. Paraphrasing gives the other person an opportunity to hear his or her message stated in different words and lets him or her know how well you understood it. Perception checking lets the other person know that you are sensitive to what he or she is feeling (and not so much to the actual content of his or her message). Summarizing communicates your overall understanding of the message and also helps both of you balance the rest of your discussion.

To use acknowledging and responding effectively:

- Restate in your own words the message you just heard ("What I hear you saying is that the issue is . . ." "In other words, you're saying that . . .").
- Reflect only the key content or points of the message.
- State your perception of your interlocutor's feelings ("You seem angry about it.").
- Pay attention to his or her nonverbal signs.
- Use empathy (be understanding).
- Restate the main themes and feelings expressed over a longer portion of the discussion ("Let me take a few minutes to recap what we've discussed so far.").
- Use summarizing to bring a part of the conversation to a close ("Before we go on to the next item on the agenda, let me summarize what we've talked about so far.").
- Use it as a bridge to the next topic of discussion.
- Avoid expressing either approval or disapproval of the person's feelings. Feelings are facts to the other person. Avoid saying, "You have a right to be angry" or "You shouldn't get so upset."
- Listen for words expressing direct feeling ("This really burns me up.") or for implied feelings ("She should have known better than that.").
- Ask yourself how you would be feeling in the other person's shoes.

One additional critical note. It is important to use these acknowledging and responding skills when you are about to engage in a conversation with someone with whom you are going to disagree. When you disagree the person often feels that you didn't listen. If you had listened, how could you possibly have disagreed?

The fact is that people do disagree. However, if you do not acknowledge the content and feeling of his or her message, *the other person will not listen to you in return.* As Steven Covey, author of *The Seven Habits of Highly Effective People* (New York: Simon & Schuster, 1989), states "seek first to understand, then to be understood."

All you have been reading so far defines what is called "active listening." It is a process of letting the other person know that you have been paying attention to and been interested in his or her thoughts and opinions. In return, he or she will usually do likewise. This is known as "mutuality" (both people engaged in the process of actively listening and exchanging information). It is a great feeling and will help you improve your communication skills.

CHAPTER 4

PRACTICE MAKES COMMUNICATING EASIER

There are any number of typical situations in which you must communicate on a daily basis: communicating problem situations, positive feedback, criticism, communicating with your boss, with peers, and with subordinates. What follows are exercises and techniques for communicating in the workplace—all based on what you have learned in the preceding chapters.

COMMUNICATING PROBLEM SITUATIONS

The goal in communicating problem situations is to be specific about the problem, so the person understands clearly what you are talking about, and in a noncriticizing way, so the person can focus on solving the problem rather than becoming defensive.

To be specific you should:

- Describe what you expected (i.e., what should be happening or the desired behavior).
- Describe what you observed and in what respect it is different from what you expected.
- Ask why it occurred.
- After asking why, stop talking and listen to the response.

DON'T LET YOURSELF GET CARRIED AWAY

When communicating about a problem, don't speak in a shouting tone, jab your finger at the person, or scowl. Use a moderate tone and open gestures, and maintain a relaxed posture.

Techniques for Being Specific

Don't Say	Do Say
"I'm really angry at you—you're in trouble."	"I have some concerns about . . ."
"I enjoy working with you, but your sloppiness annoys me."	"Four of the reports you've given me had errors in them."
"How many times were you late this week?"	"You arrived late three times this week."
"Being late with the report isn't a problem."	"Missing the deadline on the report is unacceptable."
"You'd better get with it, or else."	"You've been talking a lot lately about the amount of work you have to do."
"This will never do."	"Please rewrite this memo to include the following: . . ."
"You're sloppy."	"This letter has 5 typos."

To be noncriticizing you should:

- Avoid criticizing the person; focus on the behavior exhibited instead.
- Avoid being sarcastic or parental.
- Avoid using vague or general statements.
- Avoid using anger.
- Avoid leading with a positive, then attacking.
- Don't avoid bringing up the situation.
- Avoid asking questions for which you already know the answer.

Techniques for Being Noncriticizing

Don't Say	Do Say
"You're supposed to be on time."	"You agreed to be here at 12:00."
"You've got a bad attitude."	"You arrived here at 12:30."
"You're always late."	"Why were you late?"
"I don't want to hear your excuses."	"What happened to cause you to be late?"

EXERCISE: COMMUNICATING THE PROBLEM SITUATION

This exercise will give you an opportunity to practice communicating with a person about a problem situation. Describe how you would communicate each situation in a specific and noncriticizing way. Include what you expected, what you observed, and ask why or what happened.

Situation #1: One of your peers was supposed to get a report to you by Tuesday morning, a report that you will need to review with your boss Wednesday afternoon. The report was to contain budget projections for a project you are working on together and a summary of the activity taken to date on the project. You have completed your portion of the report. You try to call the person Tuesday afternoon, but he or she is in a meeting. Wednesday morning, you get the report from your coworker—without the budget projections.

How would you communicate this situation to your coworker in a specific and noncriticizing way?

_____
_____
_____

Situation #2: You have an old relic of a machine in your department that has required special parts for the last few years in order to keep running. Your boss has always allotted extra money in the budget to cover these parts but has not given enough to buy a new machine. Things have been tight lately. The new budget was just issued with no money set aside for your critical machine. You need to begin problem solving with your boss.

How will you communicate the problem situation?

_____
_____
_____

COMMUNICATING POSITIVE FEEDBACK

The purpose of communicating positive feedback is to acknowledge achievements. Positive feedback is valuable because it helps people understand why their efforts were important.

There are three steps to communicating positive feedback: share observations, describe the impact and value of behaviors, and show appreciation.

SHARE OBSERVATIONS

Just as when communicating problem situations, it is important for the person to know what situation or behaviors you are talking about. To share observations you should:

- Describe what you observed.
- Describe how it differed from what was expected.
- Use specific language and examples.

Techniques for Sharing Observations

Don't Say	Do Say
"You did a great job." Or, "It was better than usual."	"You finished the job in two hours and it normally takes three."

When was the last time you gave five positive reinforcements in one day? Using this technique will allow you to give as much positive reinforcement as deserved.

Describe the Impact and Value of Behaviors

Describing the impact and value of behaviors is the most important step in the positive feedback process. Without letting someone know the impact of their positive behavior on others, on the organization, or on you, the positive feedback may appear hollow. With this step, you can give the same person multiple positive strokes during the day and they will have a strong and meaningful effect. To describe the impact you should:

- Describe what happened as a result of the person's positive behavior.
- Describe the impact of the behavior on other people, resources, or processes.
- Use specific language and examples.

Techniques for Describing Impact

Don't Say	Do Say
"It really has some value."	"That means we don't have to catch up anymore by working after hours."
"People were really happy about it."	"Joe, Sue, and Steve all commented on how your efforts really helped them get their projects done faster."

Give some additional examples of positive impact statements:

_____

_____

_____

Show Appreciation

The final step to maximizing the impact of positive feedback is to let the other person know that you personally appreciate his or her efforts. To show appreciation you should:

A good job is a good job is a good job. Tell the person what was good about it.

- Give a verbal or written thank you.
- Give some public recognition of their efforts.

Techniques for Showing Appreciation

Don't Say	Do Say
"Good job, good job."	"Thank you very much for your extra effort."

EXERCISE: GIVING POSITIVE FEEDBACK

For each of the following three situations, describe how you will communicate positive feedback.

Don't forget to:

- Describe what you observed and how it differed from what was expected (i.e., communicate the positive).
- Describe the impact and value of what happened.
- Express your appreciation for the person's behavior.

Situation #1: Your department just went over the top in the United Way campaign. All the other units had been struggling because of the economic downturn. Your department now looks great in the eyes of the "big boss." Chris was responsible for the entire campaign and worked mostly after hours getting the job done.

What will you say to Chris to give positive feedback?

_____

_____

_____

_____

_____

Situation #2: Pat was able to redesign a process to manufacture toys more efficiently. The company was thinking about abandoning the project because of the expense of the "old" way of having to manufacture the toys. This new line of toys could mean a lot more money for the company. Pat not only saved the company some lean times but saved the possible loss of jobs.

What will you say to Pat to give positive feedback?

_____

_____

_____

_____

_____

Situation #3: You got in to the office early this morning expecting to have to clean up the mess from a late-night project that you and your coworkers just managed to finish before deadline. When you arrived, you discovered that Jack had come in early and cleaned up the mess.

What will you say to Jack to give positive feedback?

_____

_____

_____

_____

_____

Give some additional examples of showing appropriate appreciation:

_____

_____

_____

_____

When giving positive feedback inside the work environment, look for opportunities to recognize outstanding performance in everyone . . . not just the "star" performers but also the middle- and lower-level people. All individuals have the capacity to do outstanding work if given frequent doses of positive feedback.

COMMUNICATING CRITICISM

Most people don't do bad things intentionally. Mistakes usually happen as a result of a miscommunication about either goals and desired outcomes or process and procedures. Just letting a person know the consequences of his or her behavior is usually enough to change it. How you communicate the impact of these consequences will depend upon the amount of guilt you want to lay at their feet.

To communicate criticism you should:

- Describe the specific behavior you observed (sounds familiar?).
- Describe the impact of the behavior on others in the working environment.
- Share your personal feelings about the situation. Are you angry, sad, frustrated? Do this to expose the impact the behavior had on you personally.
- Describe the consequences of the behavior. It is important to help the person see what type of consequences it might have for him or her personally over a period of time.
- Reach an agreement on how to change behavior. This is where the rubber meets the road. If, after being made aware of the negative impact and consequences of the behavior, the person chooses to not change, then he or she is either an intentional trouble maker or under severe emotional strain. Proper disciplinary action (or counseling) should then be taken. If the person agrees to modify his or her behavior, then a process should be agreed upon to provide supportive and positive feedback.

Techniques for Communicating Criticism

Don't Say	Do Say
"When you're late, people get upset."	"By you coming in to work 30 minutes late, Jim over there has to pick up your slack and it puts extra pressure on others as well."
"If you don't change your attitude, you're going to be in big trouble."	"People are not going to want to be so cooperative with you the next time you ask for help on your project." Or, "If you continue to ignore suggestions from Jane, it will have a negative impact on your performance appraisal."

You communicate criticism to help them become aware of the negative effects of their behaviors on others and to prompt them to change . . . by creating guilt.

COMMUNICATING WITH YOUR BOSS

Companies, like all parts of society, have a built-in hierarchy of authority. Communicating up the chain of command is sometimes difficult because you may feel that your fate is in the hands of your boss. If you mess up, you're in trouble; if you appear too threatening, you're in trouble; if you come across too strong or too weak, you're in trouble. What are you to do?

Not all bosses are all-knowing. It becomes important, therefore, for you to "manage" your communications with them. To manage your communications with your boss, you should:

- Seek to clarify goals and objectives.
- Seek to clarify roles and responsibilities.
- Determine timelines (who is going to do what by when).
- Ask for feedback.
- Listen attentively.

EXERCISE: COMMUNICATING CRITICISM

Choose an individual whose behavior you are anticipating you will have to criticize. Follow these steps:

1. What was the specific behavior you observed?

   _____
   _____
   _____
   _____

2. Describe the impact of the behavior on yourself and others.

   _____
   _____
   _____
   _____

3. How do you feel about the behavior?

   _____
   _____
   _____
   _____

4. What kind of consequences might the person experience if his or her behavior doesn't change?

   _____
   _____
   _____
   _____

5. What agreements about behavior change would you like to reach?

   _____
   _____
   _____
   _____

What other ideas do you have for managing the communication process with your boss?

_____

_____

_____

_____

_____

Techniques for Communicating With Your Boss

Don't Say	Do Say
"That's his or her job, not mine."	"If our objective is to . . . then I see my responsibilities as . . . . Do you agree?"
"We'll all work hard to get things done."	"I will do (what) by (when)."

COMMUNICATING WITH PEERS

Peer communication may appear the easiest since there are minimal power struggles taking place (you're usually at the same place on the totem pole). Communication problems do arise, however, based on conflicts over resources (too few to go around), priorities (especially if you're in different departments), styles (toxic relationships), and level of perceived commitment to common goals.

To effectively communicate with a peer you should:

- Clarify your responsibilities and determine where they may overlap with your peer's.
- Identify the resources you will need to get your job done.
- Negotiate with your peer if any conflicts arise.
- Offer feedback and assistance as needed to create a positive working relationship with him or her. Network. Help each other out.

What other advice would you offer to enhance peer communications?

_____

_____

_____

_____

_____

Techniques for Communicating With Peers

Don't Say	Do Say
"You do your work and I'll do mine."	"Here is where I see our work overlapping. How should we resolve these differences to make sure both of our jobs get done?"
"It is important that my project is fully funded . . . even if it costs you resources."	"Is there something I can do to help you achieve your objectives?"

COMMUNICATING WITH SUBORDINATES

Communicating down the chain of command may appear easy, but it isn't. Whether you like it or not, as a "boss" or manager you're perceived to be in a position of power over the lives of others. "Subordinates" do things on the job to both please you and to accomplish the tasks that they think you want them to do. This is where miscommunication can have the most negative effects. To create a clear line of communication you should:

- Establish both formal and informal ways of passing along information. This can be through internal newsletters, scheduled or spontaneous meetings, or even "whiteboards" in the hall where people can write down thoughts, opinions, or messages to each other.

- Make sure you communicate your goals and objectives clearly.
- Involve others in the determination of their assignments.
- Allow another person to make decisions that will impact his or her work. You can clearly communicate the limits (and rationale) of resources, timelines, quality, and so on, but let him or her make the decisions within these limits.
- Provide continuous feedback. Don't be a stranger. People appreciate direct communication from their boss more than from any other people.
- Constantly be on the lookout for conflicts or misunderstandings and resolve them immediately.
- Listen actively and respond empathetically.

What other suggestions do you have to improve communication "down the line"?

_____

_____

_____

_____

_____

Techniques for Communicating With Subordinates

Don't Say	Do Say
"Here is what I would like for you to accomplish and this is how I want you to do it."	"Here is what I would like for you to accomplish. Think about it and tell me how you are going to achieve success."
"Boys will be boys . . . you two fight it out."	"I understand you and Joan have had a misunderstanding. How can I help?"

How to Speak and Listen Effectively has laid the foundation for effective communication. You have explored the reasons why people don't communicate better, the natural barriers to effective communication, and techniques for sending and receiving clear messages. You have also discovered methods for becoming more sensitive to the communication needs of others while applying these skills to specific work-related applications.

The rest is up to you. As with any tool box, the tools are only effective if you use them. If you choose to let them collect dust, the tools will become rusty and fall apart. The more you practice using them, however, the more effective you will become at interpersonal communication and the more other people will enjoy working with you.

Try out these tools and techniques for about three months. Then, take the self-evaluation that opened this book once again so that you can discover where you have improved—and if there are still areas that require more work.

EFFECTIVE COMMUNICATION SELF-EVALUATION

How have your communication habits, improved? Complete this communication self-evaluation by checking either "Strongly Disagree," "Disagree," "Neutral," "Agree," or "Strongly Agree" for each statement. Refer to page 00 for the scoring and interpretation grid.

	Strongly Disagree	Disagree	Neutral	Agree	Strongly Agree
1. I tend not to listen to people with whom I disagree.	☐	☐	☐	☐	☐
2. I find it difficult to fully participate in conversations where the subject is not of interest to me.	☐	☐	☐	☐	☐
3. When I feel I know the message the talker is trying to get across, I stop listening.	☐	☐	☐	☐	☐
4. I find it easy to listen to others' views even if they are different from my own.	☐	☐	☐	☐	☐
5. I ask people to clarify things I don't understand.	☐	☐	☐	☐	☐
6. I usually form a rebuttal in my head while the other person is talking.	☐	☐	☐	☐	☐
7. I often look as if I'm listening when, in fact, I'm not.	☐	☐	☐	☐	☐
8. I sometimes daydream when I should be listening.	☐	☐	☐	☐	☐

(continues)

	Strongly Disagree	Disagree	Neutral	Agree	Strongly Agree
9. If I'm not listening, I will tell the person.	☐	☐	☐	☐	☐
10. I listen for the main ideas, not the details.	☐	☐	☐	☐	☐
11. I recognize that words mean different things to different people.	☐	☐	☐	☐	☐
12. If I don't like or believe the other person, I block out what is being said.	☐	☐	☐	☐	☐
13. I look at the person who is talking.	☐	☐	☐	☐	☐
14. I concentrate on the other person's message rather than on physical appearance.	☐	☐	☐	☐	☐
15. I know which words and phrases cause me to react emotionally.	☐	☐	☐	☐	☐
16. I preplan my communications with others to accomplish my goals.	☐	☐	☐	☐	☐
17. I anticipate others' reactions to my communications.	☐	☐	☐	☐	☐
18. I take into consideration how others want to receive my information.	☐	☐	☐	☐	☐

		Strongly Disagree	Disagree	Neutral	Agree	Strongly Agree
19.	I try to determine the mood of the other person (angry, frustrated, worried, etc.) when communicating with them.	☐	☐	☐	☐	☐
20.	I feel that I am able to communicate my ideas to others so that they understand my meaning.	☐	☐	☐	☐	☐
21.	I often feel others should have known my meaning.	☐	☐	☐	☐	☐
22.	I am able to receive negative feedback without getting defensive.	☐	☐	☐	☐	☐
23.	I practice my listening skills on a regular basis.	☐	☐	☐	☐	☐
24.	I find it hard to concentrate on what someone is saying when there are noise distractions.	☐	☐	☐	☐	☐
25.	I often judge the content of others' messages when they're communicating with me.	☐	☐	☐	☐	☐
26.	I restate information given to me to make sure that I understand it correctly.	☐	☐	☐	☐	☐
27.	I let others know that I recognize the emotional level they are at when speaking to them.	☐	☐	☐	☐	☐

SELECTED READINGS

Burley-Allen, Madelyn. *Listening: The Forgotten Skill*. New York: John Wiley & Sons, 1982.

Bolton, Robert. *People Skills*. Englewood Cliffs, N.J.: Prentice Hall, 1979.

Covey, Stephen. *The Seven Basic Habits of Highly Effective People*. Provo, Utah: Institute for Principle-Centered Leadership, 1990.

Covey, Stephen. *The Principle-Centered Leader*. New York: Summit Books, 1991.

Gordon, Thomas. *Leader Effectiveness Training*. New York: Bantam, 1984.

Keirsey, David and Bates, Marilyn. *Please Understand Me*. England: Prometheus Nemesis, 1978.

Lynch, Dudley. *Your High-Performance Business Brain*. Englewood Cliffs, N.J.: Prentice-Hall, 1984.

Ohmae, Kenichi. *The Mind of the Strategist*. New York: Penguin Books, 1982.

Robbins, Harvey. *Turf Wars: Moving from Competition to Collaboration*. Glenview, Ill.: Scott-Foresman, 1990.

Rogers, Carl. *Client-Centered Therapy*. New York: Houghton-Mifflin, 1951.

Schaeffer, Robert. *The Breakthrough Strategy*. New York: Harper & Row, 1988.

Thomsett, Michael. *The Little Black Book of Business Speaking.* New York: AMACOM, 1989.

Woodcock, Mike and Francis, Dave. *Unblocking Your Organization.* United Kingdom: Gower Publishing Co., 1990.

NOTES

NOTES

NOTES

NOTES

NOTES

NOTES

NOTES

NOTES